RECONSTRUCTION
and the RISE *of*
JIM CROW

1864–1896

RECONSTRUCTION

and the RISE *of* JIM CROW

1864–1896

Christopher Collier
James Lincoln Collier

BENCHMARK BOOKS

MARSHALL CAVENDISH
NEW YORK

ACKNOWLEDGMENT: The authors wish to thank Michael Les Benedict, Professor of History, The Ohio State University, for his careful reading of the text of this volume of The Drama of American History and his thoughtful and useful comments. The work has been much improved by Professor Benedict's notes. The authors are deeply in his debt, but, of course, assume full responsibility for the substance of the work, including any errors that may appear.

Photo research by James Lincoln Collier.
COVER PHOTO: © Joslyn Art Museum
PICTURE CREDITS: The photographs in this book are used by permission and through the courtesy of:
Corbis-Bettman: 10 (left), 10 (right), 15, 17, 22, 26, 32, 36, 37, 38, 39, 42, 44, 46, 49, 50, 51, 53, 59, 60, 61, 64, 65, 66, 68, 72, 78, 80, 82, 84, 85. Library of Congress: 11, 12, 27, 30, 76. Colonial Williamsburg Foundation: 25. Independence National Historic Park: 56.

Benchmark Books
Marshall Cavendish Corporation
99 White Plains Road
Tarrytown, New York 10591-9001

©2000 Christopher Collier and James Lincoln Collier

Library of Congress Cataloging-in-Publication Data

Collier, Christopher, date
Reconstruction and the rise of Jim Crow, 1864–1896 by Christopher Collier and James Lincoln Collier.
p.   cm.   — (The drama of American history)
Includes bibliographical references and index.
Summary: Describes the struggles following the Civil War to decide how to deal with the newly-freed slaves, through the years of Reconstruction, Jim Crow, sharecropping, and segregation.
ISBN 0-7614-0819-3
1. Afro-Americans—Civil rights—Southern States—History—19th century—Juvenile literature.
2. Reconstruction—Southern States—Juvenile literature. 3. Afro-Americans—History—1863–1877—Juvenile literature. 4. Afro-Americans—History—1877–1964—Juvenile literature. 5. Afro-Americans—Segregation—Southern States—History—19th Century—Juvenile literature. 6. Southern States—Race relations—Juvenile literature. [1. Reconstruction. 2. Afro-Americans—History—1863–1877. 3. Afro-Americans—History—1877–1964. 4. Afro-Americans—Civil rights. 5. Race relations.]
I. Collier, James Lincoln, date. II. Title. III. Series: Collier, Christopher, date. Drama of American history.
E185.61.C69 2000   98-8821
975'.00496073—dc21   CIP
                                                                  AC

Printed in Italy

1 3 5 6 4 2

CONTENTS

PREFACE

Over many years of both teaching and writing for students at all levels, from grammar school to graduate school, it has been borne in on us that many, if not most, American history textbooks suffer from trying to include everything of any moment in the history of the nation. Students become lost in a swamp of factual information, and as a consequence lose track of how those facts fit together and why they are significant and relevant to the world today.

In this series, our effort has been to strip the vast amount of available detail down to a central core. Our aim is to draw in bold strokes, providing enough information, but no more than is necessary, to bring out the basic themes of the American story, and what they mean to us now. We believe that it is surely more important for students to grasp the underlying concepts and ideas that emerge from the movement of history, than to memorize an array of facts and figures.

The difference between this series and many standard texts lies in what has been left out. We are convinced that students will better remember the important themes if they are not buried under a heap of names, dates, and places.

In this sense, our primary goal is what might be called citizenship education. We think it is critically important for America as a nation and Americans as individuals to understand the origins and workings of the public institutions that are central to American society. We have asked ourselves again and again what is most important for citizens of our democracy to know so they can most effectively make the system work for them and the nation. For this reason, we have focused on political and institutional history, leaving social and cultural history less well developed.

This series is divided into volumes that move chronologically through the American story. Each is built around a single topic, such as the Pilgrims, the Constitutional Convention, or immigration. Each volume has been written so that it can stand alone, for students who wish to research a given topic. As a consequence, in many cases material from previous volumes is repeated, usually in abbreviated form, to set the topic in its historical context. That is to say, students of the Constitutional Convention must be given some idea of relations with England, and why the Revolution was fought, even though the material was covered in detail in a previous volume. Readers should find that each volume tells an entire story that can be read with or without reference to other volumes.

Despite our belief that it is of the first importance to outline sharply basic concepts and generalizations, we have not neglected the great dramas of American history. The stories that will hold the attention of students are here, and we believe they will help the concepts they illustrate to stick in their minds. We think, for example, that knowing of Abraham Baldwin's brave and dramatic decision to vote with the small states at the Constitutional Convention will bring alive the Connecticut Compromise, out of which grew the American Senate.

Each of these volumes has been read by esteemed specialists in its particular topic; we have benefited from their comments.

CHAPTER I

A Great War Ends and a New Conflict Begins

At three o'clock in the afternoon of April 9, 1865, a small group of men was gathered in the living room of a house in the little Virginia town of Appomattox Courthouse. They were General Ulysses S. Grant, chief of the Northern forces during the last year of the Civil War, and the charismatic Southern general, Robert E. Lee, along with their staffs. In silence they sat and watched as General Lee put his signature on a simple document, surrendering his troops to General Grant, and effectively putting an end to the most terrible war Americans have ever fought.

The terms of surrender were generous. Lee's soldiers were not to be treated as prisoners of war, but were to go home. It was springtime, planting season: If they had horses or mules they could take them home, too, so they would have animals to pull their plows. Further, General Grant would distribute to the sick and starving Confederate soldiers food from his ample supplies—the North had won the war in large measure because it had had more food, men, weapons, and clothing than the South.

The winner and the loser: At left, General Ulysses S. Grant, chief of the Union armies, in a portrait painted just after he had taken command of the Union forces. At right, the charismatic Robert E. Lee, holding field glasses during a Civil War battle.

The Civil War had wracked the nation. Some 620,000 men had died, most of them young, many of them teenagers, as much from disease as from battle. The South had seen its economy broken. Some of its most important cities were in ruins, two-thirds of its railroads destroyed, tens of thousands of farmhouses, barns, and homes had been burned, factories ripped apart by shells. In both sections of the country millions of lives had been altered irrevocably by the deaths of husbands, fathers, and sons. Many of those who survived had lost an arm, a leg, their eyes: In Mississippi one-third of the white men of military age were dead or disabled.

By the end of the war, many Southern cities were in ruins, the farms burned, the factories destroyed. Here is the small city of Hampton, Virginia, with nothing but chimneys remaining.

But serious as was the problem of rebuilding Southern farms and railroads, the nation was faced with an even more serious problem: how to deal with nearly four million human beings who had begun the war as slaves, and were now free.

At first glance, this might not seem like much of a problem: The newly freed blacks could set about doing the things they had always wanted to do but had been prevented from doing by their masters—getting married, raising families, finding work on farms or in cities, perhaps even saving money and buying farms of their own. But most things having to do with human beings are not simple, and this was so in the case

One of the hardest-hit of Southern cities was Atlanta. Near the end of the war General William Tecumseh Sherman made a sweep through Georgia, burning and destroying in order to deprive Southern troops of support. Atlanta was left in flames.

of the former slaves—now called freedmen. (African-Americans who were not slaves were called freemen.)

For one thing, there were immediate physical problems. As the Northern troops had swept through the South, tens of thousands of slaves had walked away from their plantations, effectively emancipating themselves. Many of them had clustered around the Northern army encampments, to live in unsanitary camps of their own, dependent upon the Union army to feed, clothe, and protect them. Other tens of thousands gathered in the towns and cities of the South, hoping for better jobs than picking cotton and planting rice. Yet others went in search of parents, children, husbands, and wives who had been sold away during slavery. But wherever they went, they were determined to get away from the old plantation where they had been slaves. One former slave, Patience Johnson, was asked by her mistress to stay on as a paid worker. She responded, "No, Miss, I must go, if I stay here I'll never know I am free." Patience's attitude was typical. The freedmen, said one observer, "are like a swarm of bees, all buzzing about and not knowing where to settle." Though largely on their own, these people needed help in finding adequate food, clothing, and shelter. They now had to build new lives for themselves that would be vastly different from the ones they had known.

The psychological problems for both blacks and whites, North and South, were at least as difficult. To begin with, only a tiny percentage of former slaves had any education. Under slavery it had, in most places, been illegal to educate blacks; most could neither read nor write and very few could do simple arithmetic. (It is true, of course, that a great many Southern whites were also illiterate.) The freedmen might easily be duped by unscrupulous employers into signing contracts they could not read, and accepting accountings they could not add up for themselves. Many of the newly freed slaves had unrealistically high hopes that they would be able to acquire their own farms, good jobs, good clothing, and have money to buy necessities and perhaps a little to jingle in their pockets.

These hopes were unrealistic partly because in the ruined South nobody, black or white, was going to have much money to jingle in his pockets, or let alone pockets to jingle anything in. But their hopes were unrealistic largely because of the way whites, who made up a majority of Southerners, perceived the situation. White Southerners strongly felt the sting of defeat. They had begun the Civil War believing that any Southerner could whip ten Yankees. After some early victories they were convinced that they were invincible. Now they had been beaten, indeed nearly destroyed, by the hated Northerners. It hurt; it hurt badly.

But white Southerners were hurt even worse by the thought that the despised blacks among them were now to be their political equals—with all the rights of citizenship—or as the saying among blacks went, "the bottom rail on top." Most Southern whites honestly believed that African-Americans were an inferior sort of humans, childlike people who could not really think for themselves, plan for the future, make intelligent choices about politics. Southern whites somewhat illogically believed on one hand that the freedpeople would always have to be cared for by whites, but on the other, feared that they might "rise in violent vengeance." And now, suddenly, Southerners were going to be forced to accept these "lesser humans" as their equals. It made them bitter and angry to think so, and many were determined not to let it happen.

Attitudes among Northerners were just as conflicted and emotional. Some, like General Grant and President Abraham Lincoln, who understood just how awful the war had been, felt a great deal of compassion for the South, and wanted to heal the wounds wrought by the war as quickly as possible. Others, however, especially those who had lost sons and brothers to Southern bullets, wanted revenge, wanted to see the South suffer for its sins. Yet others, especially businessmen, were concerned about rebuilding the South to make it a good business partner to the North.

Opinions about the place of African-Americans in the new order of things were equally diverse. The early Northern Civil War aims had been to preserve the Union. But in Northern minds there had always been the idea that slavery was an evil institution that probably ought to be ended. Lincoln, in his famous Gettysburg Address, referred to "a new birth of freedom" and a nation dedicated to the idea that "all men are created equal," suggesting that the Northern war aims had been changed to include the ending of slavery. In 1863 he issued the Emancipation

Proclamation freeing thousands of slaves—all those who had emancipated themselves by running away, those who lived in Rebel areas occupied by Union troops, and those in Union-held areas whose masters were still in rebellion. (For the story of Lincoln and the Civil War, see the volume in this series called *The Civil War*.) Long before the war was over everybody knew that a Northern victory would mean the end of slavery.

But what else would it mean for blacks? Many Northerners agreed with white Southerners that blacks were an inferior people, who could be raised up by education, but probably only so far. Such people felt that it might be right to end the evil institution of slavery, but they did not want

An artist's version of President Abraham Lincoln reading the Emancipation Proclamation, freeing certain slaves, to his cabinet ministers.

to go much beyond that. What was the point of giving blacks the vote if they could not understand the issues, they felt.

Most Northerners believed that as free people, the former slaves should be entitled to the same basic rights as white citizens. This meant especially the right to marry and have families, to acquire property, to make contracts, to earn a living, to be protected and treated fairly by law enforcement agencies. But many in the North were not yet ready to grant freedmen the right to vote or hold office, which are not necessarily rights of citizens; women, for instance, were citizens but could not vote. It is probably safe to say that less than a majority of white men in the North wanted to see African-Americans living in complete equality with whites.

Some way to bring real civil rights to the freed blacks must be found. Such people demanded that the U.S. government force the conquered Southerners to bring their former slaves up to true equality.

There were, thus, even in the North, several different ideas about what to do about the freedmen. These various opinions were reflected in Congress. At the time of Lee's surrender to Grant there were no Southerners in Congress, nor any elsewhere in the Northern government, except for a very few who had remained loyal to the Union, like Lincoln's vice president, Andrew Johnson, about whom we shall hear a good deal later in this book.

In the North, the Republican Party was dominant, although there were plenty of Democrats, too. The Republicans had control of Congress. Like everyone else, Republican congressmen had a lot of opinions about how former slaves should be treated. However, they generally divided into two groups, radicals and moderates. The radical Republicans wanted nothing short of a social revolution in the South. They wanted to see the wealthy old Southern aristocrats, who had pretty much run things in the South for generations, thrown out of power. They wanted to see African-Americans treated the same as whites. Radicals hoped that the large plantations could be divided up, and every black family be given "forty acres and a mule" to start off fresh with. The South had very few public schools, while the Northern states—especially in New England—had developed effective public school systems. The radicals wanted to see the Southern states build schools, partly to see that blacks were educated, and partly because it would be for the general good of the South. All of these schemes taken together would indeed amount to a social revolution.

The moderates were of a different opinion. They wanted the end of slavery, of course, and they wanted the freedmen to have a chance

With the end of the war, millions of blacks, now free, had to establish new lives. Many of them began drifting about the countryside, looking for work. This woodcut, from about 1870, shows a black man walking along a railroad line as part of the migration of many freedmen into Louisiana and Texas.

for better lives. But they were also eager to see the rebellious Southern states brought back into the Union as soon as possible. Further, they believed that by long-standing tradition, state governments ought to have the major say in all their own affairs. The moderates believed that in matters such as dealing with the freedmen, building schools, and dividing up the big estates, the state governments should be allowed to do as they thought best. We need to keep this split in the Republican Party firmly in mind, for throughout the years following the Civil War these two camps, who between them controlled Congress, would be forced to compromise with each other again and again in the whole problem of "reconstructing" the South.

This book, then, is the story of *Reconstruction*—the effort to reconstruct the South after the Civil War, to make it once again a prosperous and effective part of the United States of America.

Actually, Reconstruction began long before the Civil War ended. By 1863, Northern troops had captured Tennessee, the Georgia and South Carolina Sea Islands, New Orleans and other portions of Louisiana, and bits and pieces of other Southern states. Arkansas and parts of Virginia were also under Union control long before the war was over. Some sort of government had to be set up for these Southern areas captured by the North. President Lincoln was eager to bring the strayed sheep back into the fold as soon as possible, to draw them out of the enemy camp. He therefore worked out a very lenient plan of readmission, which said that when 10 percent of the voters of a state had taken an oath of allegiance to the Union, the state could send representatives to Congress in Washington, provided, of course, they agreed to end slavery. Lincoln was promising more than he could give here, for according to the Constitution it is up to Congress to accept or reject representatives and senators sent from the states. But Lincoln assumed that Congress would go along with him, as it had been doing, during the war.

But by 1865, as the war was winding down, Lincoln himself was beginning to have second thoughts about his lenient policy toward the South. The radicals especially were protesting that Southerners could not be trusted to treat the freedman fairly. In their view, the Union government would have to take strong measures to see that African-Americans got fair play. Lincoln was torn: He felt a great deal of sympathy toward the badly battered South; on the other hand, he feared that Southerners would treat the freedpeople badly.

While he was deciding what to do, Congress took steps itself. In March 1865, while Lee was making a last desperate attempt to escape the jaws of Grant's forces closing around him, Congress set up the Bureau of Refugees, Freedmen, and Abandoned Lands, known as the Freedmen's Bureau. We shall look at the workings of the Freedmen's Bureau a little later. But before it could be got up and running, fate stepped in.

There was in Washington that April an actor named John Wilkes Booth. He had grown up in Maryland, and strongly favored the South. A hatred of Lincoln, whom Booth believed was a tyrant trying to make himself king, festered in him. Booth started organizing a small group to kidnap Lincoln, or even kill him. When some of his fellow conspirators backed out, Booth determined to kill Lincoln himself.

A few days after Lee's surrender, it became known that Lincoln would go to the Ford Theater to see a popular play called *Our American Cousin*. The date was April 14, which happened to be Good Friday. As a well-known actor, Booth was easily able to get into the theater and go upstairs, until he was standing directly behind Lincoln's box. At 10:13 p.m. he slipped into the box, pointed a small derringer at the president's head and fired from a distance of two feet. Lincoln slumped forward. Booth leaped from the box onto the stage. In so doing he caught his foot in one of the flags decorating Lincoln's box and fell on one foot, breaking a bone in his leg. Nonetheless, he rose to his feet, shouted, "Sic semper tyrannis" ("Thus always to tyrants"), and fled. Lincoln was carried to a nearby house, unconscious. He never regained consciousness, and

Andrew Johnson, who became president when Lincoln was assassinated, tended to be arrogant, and lacked Lincoln's diplomatic skills. Had Lincoln lived, the nation's wounds might have healed sooner.

Party to accommodate the Democrat Johnson. And so, by chance, a Southerner, not a Northerner, would preside over the Reconstruction of the South.

Andrew Johnson was in many ways the exact opposite of Lincoln. Where Lincoln was a good politician, able to cajole people around to his way of thinking, and compromise with them when he couldn't, Johnson was stubborn, egotistical, determined to get his way. Where Llincoln was charitable toward his enemies, Johnson was vindictive, out ot get an eye for an eye. Where Lincoln could put himself in the shoes of other people, Johnson's character and approach appealed to the ordinary Tennessee farmers who voted for him.

Most importantly, where Lincoln had always hated slavery, Johnson was of two minds about it. Early in his life he had shown little concern for blacks. As governor of Tennessee, however, he sympathized with their plight as long as they remained in slavery there—which they did until the Thirteenth Amendment outlawing slavery was ratified in 1865. Johnson disliked slavery most because it put the slaveholders at such a great advantage over the ordinary farmer who could not afford to buy slaves. He came to the presidency a man whose concern for African-Americans was halfhearted at best. From the outset, then, Andrew Johnson was not in tune with the ideas of the Republicans who controlled Congress—especially the radicals, who would soon dominate there.

Johnson adopted—with some significant changes—Lincoln's lenient "10 percent plan" for Southern Reconstruction, under which a state could rejoin the Union when 10 percent of its voters took an oath of loyalty to the Union. Johnson's version of the plan required 50 percent of the voters to take the loyalty oath and also required the states to ratify the Thirteenth Amendment to the Constitution abolishing slavery. But Johnson did not favor giving the vote to any black Americans.

This lenient approach was acceptable to a surprisingly large number of Northerners, even many who had fought in the war. To repeat, even after the Civil War most Americans believed that the U.S. government ought not have much direct authority over people: Most everyday matters ought to be left to the states. Few Americans believed that politicians in Washington ought to decide who would govern in the Southern states. Even Lincoln had said, "We can't undertake to run State governments in all those Southern States. The people must do that—though I reckon that at first some of them may do it badly."

So the Southern states set about reconstructing themselves. President Johnson appointed temporary governors in each state. The governors called for state conventions to write new constitutions for their states. Certain categories of Southerners, like people who had been major office-holders in the Confederacy, would not be allowed to vote for delegates, unless they swore allegiance to the Union and were pardoned by the president. In effect most whites could vote for delegates. Blacks, however, could not. The conventions were held, new constitutions were written, and soon new governments existed in all Southern states. In December

1865 the Southern states sent representatives and senators to Congress. Johnson expected them to be allowed to take their seats there. As far as he was concerned, the Southern states were accepted back into the Union.

Now these state governments set about turning the freedmen as much as they could back into near slavery through a whole series of laws that came to be known as the Black Codes. These laws were meant to prevent African-Americans from achieving equality and keep them in a state of subservient social standing. But another important objective was to make sure that the black population of the South would continue to serve as cheap labor on the plantations to keep the economy running.

Under the Black Codes, blacks could not work where and when they wanted to, but were required to sign labor contracts with plantation owners. If they left the job before the contract was up they could be arrested. They could also be arrested under "vagrancy laws" simply for not having a job. They could be arrested for making "insulting" gestures to whites, even for "misspending" their own money. Some towns and counties in South Carolina passed laws barring blacks from taking any kind of job except as servants or field hands. A Mississippi law said that "all freedmen, free Negroes and mulattos in this State over the age of eighteen . . . found unlawfully assembling themselves together, either in the day or nighttime. . . ." could be fined or arrested. A Louisiana law said that in a dispute between an employer and a worker, the employer had the right to settle the problem. In Texas the labor contract law said that it applied to the family members of the man who signed it, which means that wives would be forced to work in the fields. In Maryland and North Carolina laws said that black orphans, or black children of parents who could not support them, could be bound out as apprentices to work for nothing on plantations. Other laws prevented blacks from hunting and fishing, the idea being to keep them from making their livings any way but laboring in the fields.

Other laws banned blacks from serving on juries. Such laws made it

Johnson was driven by a hatred of the aristocratic plantation owners, who held most of the wealth and the power in the South, rather than by a desire to help blacks. The lives of wealthy planters contrasted vividly with that of the poor farmers Johnson grew up among. Here, in a reconstruction, is a typical drawing room of a wealthy Virginian.

almost impossible for blacks to sue whites or charge whites with crimes. In the first two years after the war, five hundred Texas white men were charged with murdering blacks: Not one was convicted. Conversely, a black who committed any kind of crime against a white was bound to be arrested and given a long jail sentence. In fact, Southern authorities deliberately arrested blacks on any flimsy excuse they could find. Black prisoners could be "rented" out to plantation owners, which brought money into state treasuries and provided a lot of cheap labor to cotton growers.

Some states were also taking the first steps toward a policy of "segregating" blacks from whites, a system that would eventually become the

Attacks on freedmen who would not toe the line were frequent. Here is a woodcut of the murder of a black man during a massacre of blacks in a small Southern town.

main device for keeping African-Americans second-class citizens. Town ordinances limited blacks to special streetcars. Some states permitted railroads to bar blacks from traveling in first-class coaches unless they were servants with their masters. Other states made it illegal for blacks to go to public meetings—even church services—without permission from whites.

It is true that the *legal* position of blacks was much improved from what it had been under slavery. They could get married without fear that their families would be torn away from them, they could travel, could earn money, could in some places get a little education, even sue whites on rare occasion. But in most Southern states the Black Codes left freedpeople far short of the complete freedom they expected. Though thousands of freedpeople refused to work unless they were also given their own plots to farm, and many thousands went to towns and cities to find work, many others found themselves back in the slave cabins, working from sunup to sundown, eating sparingly and following the orders of a field boss.

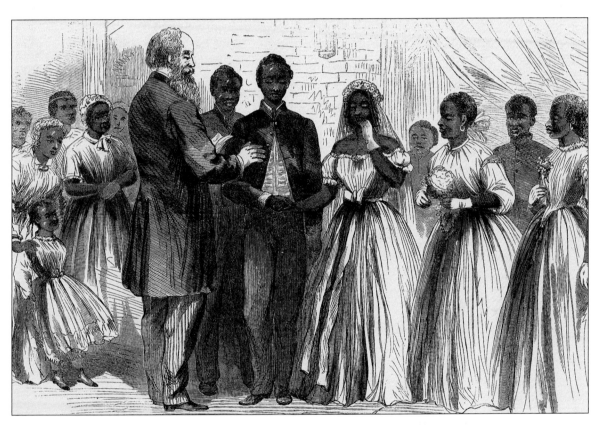

Southern black slaves had never been allowed to marry legally, although they had often performed marriage ceremonies of their own. With their freedom, many couples rushed to be legally married. The Freedmen's Bureau often arranged these marriages and supplied chaplains to perform the ceremony, as in this picture.

Fortunately for the former slaves there was the Freedmen's Bureau. This proved to be a very important organization, and probably did more to help African-Americans in their efforts to find their way in the new world of freedom than anything else Congress did for them.

The bureau was headed by General O. O. Howard, and staffed largely by Union army officers. It was thus a semimilitary body, using army funds. Over four years the Freedmen's Bureau gave twenty-one million rations of food to both black and white refugees. It established forty hospitals, and settled some thirty thousand people who had become homeless during the war. It also tried to find land for farms for blacks. This was something freedmen desperately wanted, as a way to escape from the plantation work forces. Unfortunately, President Johnson had decreed that land abandoned during the fighting had to be returned to its white owners, rather than be divided up into farms for freedmen. Besides, some towns passed local ordinances providing specifically that African-Americans could not own land. Nonetheless, the Freedmen's Bureau did manage to settle some blacks on farms of their own.

The Freedmen's Bureau was also critically important in negotiating labor agreements between the freedmen and the former slave owners. Few blacks could read, and it was necessary that somebody look over the labor contracts. The Freedmen's Bureau helped to establish fair wages and to settle disputes between workers and employers.

The bureau had its greatest successes in the field of education. It had long been believed among African-Americans that education was the path to true freedom: If you could not read or write, how could you understand your rights under the law, how could you sue, how could you know what a contract said? Blacks were eager for education. The Freedmen's Bureau created and supervised thousands of schools of various kinds, and young and old African-Americans flocked to them. The bureau also gave financial support to a number of colleges for African-Americans, among them the well-known Howard and Fisk universities.

| | POPULATION IN 1860 | | | SLAVES AT TIME OF EMANCIPATION | DATE OF RE-CONSTRUCTION | BLACKS IN RECONSTRUCTION CONVENTIONS | | DATE OF RE-ESTAB-LISHMENT OF WHITE SUPREMACY |
	White	Black	%			Number	Percent	
UNION SLAVE STATES								
Delaware	466,000	78,000	19.3	1,808				
Kentucky	919,000	236,000	20.4	225,000				
Maryland	516,000	171,000	24.9	90,000				
Missouri	1,063,000	119,000	10.0	437,000				
West Virginia	424,000*	18,000*						
CONFEDERATE SLAVE STATES								
Alabama	526,000	438,000	45.4	435,000	1868	17	17	1875
Arkansas	324,000	111,000	25.6	111,000	1868	8	13	1875
Florida	78,000	63,000	44.6	62,000	1868	19	40	1877
Georgia	592,000	466,000	44.1	462,000	1870	36	19	1871
Louisiana	357,000	350,000	49.5	332,000	1868	50	50	1877
Mississippi	354,000	437,000	55.3	437,000	1870	16	17	1875
North Carolina	630,000	362,000	36.4	331,000	1868	14	11	1871
South Carolina	291,000	412,000	58.6	402,000	1868	71	61	1877
Tennessee	827,000	283,000	25.5	276,000	1866			1871
Texas	421,000	183,000	30.3	165,000	1870	10	10	1873
Virginia	1,047,000†	549,000†	34.4	472,000	1870	24	24	1871

* For 1870   † Includes West Virginia

A quarter of a million former slaves were taught the basics of English and arithmetic through the work of the Freedmen's Bureau.

Needless to say, the bureau was royally hated by most Southerners. They viewed it as "virtually a foreign government forced upon them and supported by an army of occupation." They insisted that having bureau

African-Americans in the South had long felt that education would be the key to raising themselves up in American society. One of the most important jobs the Freedmen's Bureau did was to provide schools that eventually taught tens of thousands of blacks to read and write. Blacks of all ages attended these schools.

officials sit in judgment on cases, as if they were running courts of law, was illegal and unconstitutional.

The Black Codes could not be kept a secret, nor could the defiant attitude of many Southerners toward the North. By the time that Congress next met, in December 1865, several Southern states had put together their new governments.

The radical Republicans in Congress were aghast at the Black Codes and the fact that a lot of former officials of the Confederacy were back in office. They were outraged by acts of defiance, like the refusal of some Southern officials to fly the American flag over their statehouses. They were determined to reconstruct the South in their own way.

Moreover, during the war, Congress had seen its powers eroded under a strong president. Congressmen were ready to assert themselves against President Johnson. They began by refusing to seat the new senators and representatives sent to Washington by the Southern states, which, under the Constitution, Congress had a right to do. But there was more to it than simple revenge. The Constitution provided that only three-fifths of the slaves were counted in figuring out how many representatives each state could have. Now there were no more slaves, and the Southern states were entitled to many more representatives than before. Southern Congressmen would be mainly Democrats, and in combination with Northern Democrats, might be able to take over the House of Representatives. This the Republicans and other Unionists could not permit. Additionally, the Republicans wanted to find ways to make their party as strong in the South as it was in the North. And so the Congress began its own program of Reconstruction.

Although many Republicans did not yet realize it, in so doing they were setting themselves on a collision course with President Andrew Johnson. It is not easy to understand exactly why Johnson took the tack that he did. Some of it was his honest belief that by the traditional interpretation of the Constitution the states had to be allowed to do pretty much what they wanted to do, even when it came to enacting laws like Black Codes. Some of it was probably an underlying sympathy for the South, where he had lived all of his life. Some of it was simple stubbornness, the feeling that he was president and his ideas had to be respected.

Whatever the case, in 1866 Congress passed a routine bill extending the life of the Freedmen's Bureau, and expanding its powers. Johnson vetoed it. He explained that for one reason, the states most affected by it had no representatives in Congress, and for another, allowing the Freedmen's Bureau to act like a court in settling disputes between blacks and whites was unconstitutional. Congress rejected these arguments and passed the bill over the president's veto.

Then in April 1866 Congress passed what is known as the Civil Rights Act. Back before the Civil War, the Supreme Court, in the famous Dred Scott case, had declared that African-Americans were not citizens of the United States and that states could not make them such. The Civil Rights Act was intended to get around this decision. It said that all persons born in the United States (except Indians, who fell into a different category) were citizens and had the same civil rights. Johnson vetoed the bill, but Congress passed it over his veto.

As the celebrated black writer Frederick Douglass put it, "While the legislatures of the South retain the right to pass laws mak-

One of the most prominent African-Americans of the time was Frederick Douglass, writer and speaker. A former slave, he was able to tell Northern audiences what slavery had been like from firsthand experience.

ing any discrimination between black and white, slavery still lives there."
The Civil Rights Act was meant to make freedom real. A white supporter of black rights, Wendell Phillips, said that the goal was "absolute
equality before the law; absolute civil equality." Equality was precisely
what white Southerners did not want. It was the sticking point, and when
President Johnson vetoed the bill, a line had been crossed: The president
and Congress were at war.

CHAPTER III

The Impeachment of Andrew Johnson

The radical Republicans in Congress were now determined to ram their version of Reconstruction past President Johnson, bring about a social revolution in the South, and raise blacks to equality with whites. They were concerned that the Supreme Court might find the Civil Rights Act unconstitutional: After all, in the Dred Scott case the Court had said specifically that African-Americans were not United States citizens. The Republicans decided to amend the Constitution to wipe away the Dred Scott ruling, and make sure that the Civil Rights Act could not be ruled unconstitutional or repealed by a later Congress.

What became the Fourteenth Amendment to the U.S. Constitution was the result of a compromise by the radicals, who gave up their effort to give full voting rights to black men in exchange for a guarantee of equal civil rights for blacks. Since the end of the three-fifths clause would give Southern states additional representatives in Congress, now that *all* blacks would be included in the population count, radicals insisted that representation from the South be reduced. They also got a provision disqualifying former Rebels from holding office. The radicals reluctantly agreed to permit the congressmen from the former Confederate states to take their seats after their state ratified the Fourteenth Amendment.

The key part of what became the Fourteenth Amendment read: "All persons born or naturalized in the United States, and subject to the jurisdiction thereof, are citizens of the United States and of the State wherein they reside. No State shall make or enforce any law which shall abridge the privileges or immunities of citizens of the United States; nor shall any State deprive any person of life, liberty, or property, without due process of law; nor deny to any person within its jurisdiction the equal protection of the laws."

The central point of the Fourteenth Amendment was that state governments—whether they liked it or not—had to treat African-Americans as equal citizens. The Fourteenth Amendment was passed by Congress in June 1866, ratified by three-fourths of the states, and became part of the U.S. Constitution in July 1868. As we shall see, however, it was not effective in protecting civil rights for many years. But a century later it became the legal basis for black triumphs in the twentieth-century battle for their rights.

President Johnson, in his turn, was determined to halt the Republican Reconstruction program. He believed he would have his chance soon, for in the fall of 1866, while the Fourteenth Amendment was being considered by the states for ratification, there would be congressional elections. Johnson was confident that the American people were tired of Reconstruction, were not interested in black civil rights, disliked seeing the federal government take power away from the states, and wanted to put the bitter sectional bickering behind them. If Johnson could persuade Northern voters to return people who agreed with him to Congress, the power of the Republicans would be sharply curtailed. In August 1866 he declared that the "insurrection" was at an end. Soon the Congress would be filling up with Southern Democrats.

The Fourteenth Amendment did not immediately do much to help blacks. But a century later the lawyer Thurgood Marshall, later a Supreme Court justice, used it as the legal basis for eliminating segregation, on the grounds that "separate" was inherently "unequal."

And all this might have happened, for a good many Northerners did think that the Republicans had gone too far, and were tired of the whole business. But Johnson's arrogant and pugnacious personality got him in trouble. His belligerent speeches annoyed the press, businessmen, and many ordinary voters. On top of it, terrible race riots broke out in New Orleans and Memphis, in which many blacks were killed or injured—this helped persuade Northern voters that white Southerners would not give African-Americans fair treatment unless they were forced to. They voted for the radical Republicans overwhelmingly. In the new Congress they had not just a majority but enough votes to override presidential vetoes. The radicals hoped they could now push their program through.

At this point Johnson ought to have been realistic and find ways to compromise with the Congress. But he was stubborn, and kept trying to get around the Republicans. One way he could get the federal government off the back of the South was by curbing the power of the Union army—which still occupied much of the old Confederacy—to enforce laws passed by Congress. He brought a lot of troops home, sent others to the West to fight Indians, and replaced officers who were enforcing the laws vigorously with others who would be more lenient—who would, in effect, allow whites to intimidate blacks.

As it happened, the secretary of war was Edwin Stanton, who had been appointed by Lincoln. Stanton was on the side of the radicals, and was determined to support black rights. In July the military command issued an order saying that when Southern courts failed to try people who had committed crimes against blacks, as they frequently did, military courts could step in. In response, Johnson issued a proclamation criticizing the use of military courts to try civil cases. Then, in December

As a consequence of white efforts to keep blacks in serfdom in the South, there was much violence, with rioting between the races. Here, blacks and whites fight in the streets of Charleston, South Carolina, in 1866.

After the Civil War, Union troops stayed in the South to enforce the new laws giving blacks their rights. But Andrew Johnson decided to bring many of these troops home, which allowed Southern governments to ignore Federal rules. This picture shows Union troops on St. Louis Street in New Orleans.

1866, the Supreme Court handed down a decision in a case known as *Ex parte Milligan*, which said that military courts could not be used in area where the civil courts existed and no fighting was going on. The war, of course, was over, and there was no fighting going on anywhere. This

A cartoon from a Northern periodical shows a black voter being threatened by whites, who demand that he vote for the Democratic candidate, instead of for the Republicans, who were supporting black rights.

decision seemed to say that the military could not be used to punish people who harmed blacks or prevented them from exercising their civil rights. As the white-dominated civil courts would not punish such people, Southern whites now had a free hand to do whatever they wanted to do to blacks. The result was inevitable. Blacks who tried to vote were driven away from the polls, often beaten, and sometimes killed. Blacks who protested too loudly against such terrorism were also likely to be beaten or killed. These tactics proved successful: Not all blacks were cowed by white threats, but a great many were. In order to save their skins, they remained silent, and made the best of things as they could.

The Republicans in Congress were getting reports on the situation, often from people in the Freed-men's Bureau, most of whom were in sympathy with the freedmen. The radicals were determined to reestablish military control in the South. In 1867 Congress passed the Military

Reconstruction Act. This act divided the South into five districts, which would be run by military officers empowered to protect the rights and property of both blacks and whites and to try people who committed crimes. Furthermore, the military commanders could remove state and local officials and replace them with men of their own choice. The Military Reconstruction Act was not meant solely to protect the rights of blacks. The disruption to the South caused by the Civil War had made for a great deal of lawlessness in general. Thousands of bitter, disillusioned, hungry, and armed young Confederate veterans were loose in the countryside. Many went West, but many remained in the South as trouble-makers. There were frequent riots about various matters, all kinds of cheating during elections, and much crime. Southern authorities themselves were having trouble keeping order. Nevertheless, the Military Reconstruction Act was meant principally to protect the rights of the freedmen.

The act did not go as far as the more radical Republicans wanted: They had hoped simply to replace Southern state governments with ones more to their liking. But it went pretty far, and in compensation moderates got a provision they wanted: The states could send representatives and senators to Congress once they had accepted the Fourteenth Amendment and extended equal civil and voting rights to African-Americans. President Johnson, of course, vetoed the Military Reconstruction Act and the Congress, of course, overrode his veto.

By this time the Republican-controlled Congress had had enough of President Johnson. It appeared to many that, despite the fact that Johnson had remained loyal to the Union during the war, he was at heart a Southerner. In this many historians agree. He consistently supported Southern positions on issues, showed little interest in black civil rights, and did everything he could to get around laws passed by Congress to raise African-Americans to equality.

Yet we cannot see Andrew Johnson as just another racist. For one thing, his main passion had always been to bring down the wealthy Southern aristocrats who he believed were grinding ordinary dirt farmers under their heels. He had never really been anti-South, so much as anti-aristocrat. For another thing, in taking many of the stands he took, he pointed out that traditionally states had always had control of matters like voting, contracts, and civil rights in general. (The Fourteenth Amendment, recall, would not be ratified until July 1868.) He claimed that he was only following the ideas of the Founding Fathers. He insisted that some of the measures the Republicans were pushing through were unconstitutional, as indeed the Supreme Court eventually agreed.

The problem was not so much that Johnson's arguments were wrong, but that Southerners were using all sorts of illegal and unconstitutional actions to deprive African-Americans of anything like an equal place in Southern society. Southern governments would not enforce their own laws against fraud, assault, and even murder when the victims were black. The Republicans felt that they had no choice but to take strong measures.

Thus, from the beginning of 1867 radical Republicans were looking for ways to tie the president's hands—or get rid of him entirely. This was an unusual, indeed unprecedented, idea. Lower officials, like judges, had a few times been impeached and forced out of office. However, it was one thing to impeach a judge; it was quite another to impeach a president. The impeachment of Andrew Johnson was a very serious and unusual thing to consider. But by the time of the Military Reconstruction Act, the radical Republicans in Congress were advocating it.

We must understand that the *impeaching* of an official does not mean *convicting* him of anything. An impeachment means only that the person is *charged* with a crime, after which he can then be *tried* to see if he is guilty or innocent.

As spelled out in the Constitution, the House of Representatives has the sole right to impeach a Federal official. It can do so by a simple

American presidents have always shown a great respect for their own office, and have almost never violated their oath of office. Only twice since Andrew Johnson's time have presidents run into serious trouble. In 1974, President Richard Nixon was forced to resign to avoid impeachment. In 1998, President Bill Clinton was impeached but, like Johnson, was not convicted by the Senate and remained in office. Above is a photograph of the Clinton impeachment hearing in progress.

majority. The impeached person is then brought before the Senate for trial. Two-thirds of the senators present must vote to convict. Additionally, when the president is on trial, the chief justice of the Supreme Court must preside.

The Republicans in Congress knew that they could not get away with impeaching Johnson without a good cause. So, in March 1867 the Congress passed a bill saying that all orders to army officers had to pass through the hands of General Ulysses S. Grant, the hero who had led the Union armies to victory. Grant had never been a strong supporter of black rights, but he had, after all, sent a great many men to their death in battle to preserve the Union and end slavery. By 1867 Grant had been pushed into the Republican camp by the leniency of Johnson toward the South. The radical Republicans believed that Grant would enforce U.S. laws meant to protect blacks. But the law was a strange one, for it meant that the president, who after all was the commander in chief of the army, could not give orders to the officers under him.

More important, at the same time, Congress passed the Tenure of Office Act. The president's appointment of many government officials, like cabinet members and ambassadors, must be approved by the Senate. The Tenure of Office Act said that such officials could not be removed from office until the Senate confirmed their successors. From the beginning, under the Constitution, presidents had been firing their subordinates, even those confirmed by the Senate, without Senate approval. This new law was against an old tradition and would probably be considered unconstitutional today. President Johnson vetoed it, and once again the Congress overrode his veto.

If Johnson had swallowed hard and accepted the new laws he would have effectively given over to Congress a good portion of his powers. He would not do this, not just because he was a stubborn man but because he felt that Congress was destroying a basic principle of American government, the separation of powers—the idea that Congress and the president should be more or less equal to each other, so that each could "check" the other if it got too tyrannical. He knew that these new laws were aimed primarily at giving Congress control of who would command the army, which was supposed to be under the president's command. To challenge Congress, Johnson fired Secretary of War Edwin Stanton.

Johnson knew perfectly well that this was exactly what the radical Republicans wanted him to do, because it would give them an excuse to impeach him and persuade the moderate Republicans to go along. He went ahead with the challenge anyway, for he believed that the majority of voters in the North supported his lenient attitude toward the South. He was wrong about this. As the celebrated Union general William Tecumseh Sherman put it, "He attempts to govern after he has lost the means to govern. He is like a General fighting without an army."

As soon as Johnson fired Stanton, the Republican-dominated House of Representatives acted. It set up a committee to find reasons for impeachment. The committee quickly drew up eleven Articles of Impeachment, and just as quickly, early in March 1867, the House passed the impeachment bill. The case now went to the Senate for trial.

The case against President Johnson was flimsy. It came down to breaking the Tenure of Office Act by firing Secretary Stanton. To begin with, the Tenure of Office Act was of doubtful constitutionality. More important, the Constitution said the president could be impeached only for *high crimes and misdemeanors.* It seemed to many people that this phrase meant only really serious crimes like accepting bribes, betraying secrets to foreign powers, and using the army to strip people of their rights. But there was no evidence that Andrew Johnson had taken bribes

or made secret deals with anybody. Was breaking a dubious law like the Tenure of Office Act really a high crime or misdemeanor? Most experts on the Constitution today would probably say that

Edwin Stanton was Lincoln's secretary of war, and continued in office when Andrew Johnson took over. Johnson's firing of Stanton triggered the impeachment proceedings against him.

under the circumstances existing in 1867 it wasn't. And beyond that, Stanton had been appointed by Lincoln, not Johnson, so the Tenure of Office Act may not have applied in this case, anyway.

But the radical Republicans had a different view. They saw that Johnson was trying to upset the whole Reconstruction policy that Congress had quite legally passed. The president was clearly not enforcing the law as he had sworn to do, and he was doing what he could to get around it—and that did seem like a serious matter.

There was no question that a majority of the senators wanted Johnson out. Whether the necessary two-thirds did was another matter. Johnson had certain points on his side. For one, he had succeeded to office as Lincoln's vice president; he had no vice president of his own. He would be succeeded by the president of the Senate, Ben Wade. Wade was a strong radical Republican. A lot of people, both congressmen and voters, did not want such a radical Republican in the presidency. Wealthy businessmen and industrialists, among others, vastly preferred Johnson to Wade, because they wanted to settle matters in the South so as to do business there. (Today, under the Twenty-Fifth Amendment, a president who is without a vice president must nominate someone to the office who must then be confirmed by a majority of both houses of Congress.)

For another thing, for reasons we shall look at shortly, the Republicans were winning a lot of elections in the South, and it seemed that the party would have some control in the Southern states no matter what Johnson wanted. Finally, Johnson quietly let word go out that he would stop obstructing congressional plans for Reconstruction if he were permitted to stay in office.

When the Senate voted in May, seven Republicans voted against convicting Johnson. The final tally was one vote short of the needed two-thirds. In fact the vote was not actually as close as it looked, for several other Republicans had said that they would vote to save Johnson if necessary. In their hearts these Republicans believed that you could not jus-

The impeachment process is sometimes confusing. Impeachment means only that the officeholder is charged with a crime. The Senate must then try the person to determine his guilt or innocence. When a president is tried, the chief justice of the Supreme Court must preside. Justice Salmon P. Chase presided at the trial of Andrew Johnson.

tify impeaching a president for breaking a questionable and unimportant law like the Tenure of Office Act. So Johnson would remain as president.

Opinions about the impeachment of Andrew Johnson have changed over the years. For a long time it was believed that Johnson was right and the Republicans were wrong. In this view, Johnson was trying to forgive the rebellious Southerners as Lincoln would have wanted him to do, and put the Union back together as speedily as possible, which after all was the first reason for fighting for the war. The radical Republicans were seen as fanatics who were determined to punish the South for its sins and who used shabby tactics in their attempt to bring Johnson down.

Historians today take a different view. They see that Johnson was arrogant and self-centered, a man who had no interest in giving African-Amer-icans their full rights, or any rights at all. In addition, the radicals, historians have shown, could not have gone as far as they did without the support of the more moderate Republicans.

There is probably something to be said for both viewpoints. However, there is no doubt that Johnson was trying to thwart the radical Republicans' plans for Reconstruction, which had quite constitutionally been put into law. In this sense, Johnson was surely guilty of a serious matter. Unquestionably, some of the radicals were fanatics; but many, if not most, believed sincerely in equality for blacks.

But in the end the effort to impeach Johnson may have been counter-productive because it helped to turn people away from radical Reconstruction proposals. Although the states would ratify the Fifteenth Amendment giving the vote to black men in 1870, the tide was beginning to turn against the radicals.

CHAPTER IV

The Tide Turns

At first, it appeared that the Republicans would be able to reconstruct the Southern governments as they wished to. Under the first Reconstruction Act, the South was divided into five districts, each with a Union general in charge, supported by 20,000 Federal troops and black militiamen. The South was now really being run by military governments empowered to bring equality to blacks. These military governments made sure that African-Americans could vote, and, of course, they would vote for Republican candidates. In addition, a considerable number of people had come down from the North after the Civil War. Southerners scornfully called these Northerners "carpetbaggers," after the sort of small, cheap luggage they were supposed to have brought with them. Some of the carpetbaggers came to take advantage of the chaos in the South to enrich themselves; others came to make legitimate investments in factories and farms that might be of benefit to Southerners. But large numbers came with sincere concern for the welfare of the freedmen and hoped to help improve their lot.

Finally, Republican candidates in the Southern states got votes from

During the Recon-struction period, Federal troops took control of much of the government of Southern states. In this woodcut of 1876, Federal troops are standing guard in the state capitol building in Columbia, South Carolina.

a surprisingly large number of Southern whites. Many had never really liked secession and the Confederate government. These "scalawags," as they were called by other Southerners, were mainly poor farmers who felt that they had always been ground down by the wealthy planters. During the Civil War many of them believed that they were being asked to fight and die to preserve the power of the aristocrats. A lot of them had fled into the woods in order to avoid being taken into the Confederate army; others stayed quiet, but did as little as possible to aid the South in the war. Now, some scalawags were ready to form alliances with blacks as a way to take power away from the old plantation aristocrats.

Among all these people—the blacks who constituted majorities or large minorities in the Deep South states, the scalawags, and the carpet-baggers—the Republicans had enough votes to control many state governments. Many blacks were elected to state legislatures, to other offices, and even to Congress when Southern representatives were allowed back. By 1868 these new governments, dominated by the Republicans, had been set up in eight of the Southern states, and the remaining three were reconstructed in 1870. As soon as any of them ratified the Fourteenth Amendment and fulfilled other provisions of the Reconstruction Acts, they were readmitted to Congress, and fairly quickly the military governments were dismantled and the Northern troops were withdrawn.

These "radical" governments have come in for a lot of criticism. It is true that at times illiterate blacks were elected to state legislatures. It is

THE MAN WITH THE (CARPET) BAGS.

Typifying the carpetbagger was Carl Schurz, a distinguished writer, editor, and politician. A German immigrant who had settled in Wisconsin, Schurz moved to Missouri and was thence elected to the Senate by votes of Republicans joined by blacks, scalawags, and carpetbaggers.

also true that white scalawags and carpetbaggers sometimes manipulated naive and badly educated black officeholders for their own advantage. It is also true that some of the scalawags and carpetbaggers were corrupt: Franklin J. Moses, a carpetbag governor of South Carolina, "entirely devoid of moral sense," managed to enrich himself personally, and he was hardly alone. And it is also true that some of the military rulers at times ran roughshod over Southerners' constitutional rights.

But neither were these Reconstruction governments totally bad. Some black legislators may have been uneducated and behaved foolishly, but the majority of them had had some education and were no better or worse than the average white legislator; in any case, blacks never controlled the governments of any Southern state. Some carpetbaggers like Governor Moses were corrupt; but others brought capital and

This 1872 cartoon from the popular magazine Puck *satirized the carpetbaggers from the North appearing to bear down on the defeated and devastated South. The fact that* Puck *was a national magazine indicates that there was much sympathy for the South among Northerners as well.*

expertise into the South to help revitalize the economy, and others came to establish schools and colleges where there had been none before. Some of the military governors were careless about constitutional rights, but Reconstruction governments also started public school systems for the South, repealed the vicious Black Codes, and rebuilt public roads, bridges, and buildings. Like many things in human life, the radical governments that were instituted in the years 1868–70 were mixtures of good and bad.

They were nonetheless hated by most white Southerners, who deeply resented what they considered to be Northern control of their states, and who resented even more the sight of African-Americans not only voting and owning property but actually sitting in state legislatures making laws for them. They were bound to fight back, and they did.

The turning of the tide first became visible in the debates over what would become the Fifteenth Amendment to the Constitution, which was intended to make sure that black males had the vote. We must understand that until the twentieth century not all citizens had the right to vote. Voting was considered by many to be a privilege, not a right. To begin with, women were not allowed to vote. Neither were Indians on tribal lands. In some states only men who paid a "poll tax" could vote. In others there were literacy tests. In the West, American-born Chinese were denied the vote in the very year that the Fifteenth Amendment was ratified. And in most Northern states free blacks could not vote.

At the time of the Emancipation Proclamation in 1863, when the war was still on, few people believed that the freedmen ought to get the vote. Lincoln himself was not considering the idea. As we have seen, a great many white Americans believed that blacks were not smart enough to vote intelligently. Even those who disagreed felt that the majority of freedmen would not be ready to vote until they had received some education and an understanding of how politics worked.

But as Reconstruction began, African-American leaders like Frederick

Under Reconstruction, African-Americans were elected to both state and Federal offices. One of the best known of them was Hiram R. Revell, the first black senator. He is shown here in 1880 at the time of his admission to practice before the Supreme Court.

Douglass and their white allies came more and more to believe that the former slaves would not be truly free until they could vote. If African-Americans could vote, they reasoned, in order to get elected politicians would have to take their needs into account.

There was more to it, however. Northern Republicans wanted to build up their party in the South to make it truly a national party. Most white Southerners would no more vote for a Republican than they would vote for an African-American. If the Republican Party in the South were to exist at all, it would need black voters. In addition, a law giving freed-men the vote would also give it to blacks in the North in states where they did not have it. These blacks would certainly vote Republican and build up the party in the North as well. There were thus, for the radicals, both practical and principled reasons for making sure that African-Americans voted.

So, in 1869 Congress sent to the states for ratification the Fifteenth Amendment, which prohibited any state from depriving a citizen of the vote on the grounds of race. Some Republicans wanted to cast an even wider net with the amendment, giving the vote to all white males, thus eliminating the few restrictions some states still had based on property, literacy, and other factors. And, of course, members of the spreading women's movement wanted to have the amendment include females, too. But there were people opposed to giving the suffrage (the right to vote) to women, to Chinese immigrants and their children, and to the poor. Moreover, universal male suffrage would allow certain former rebels to vote who had been disqualified for their roles in the Confederate gov-ernment. The radical leadership knew that if it cast too broad a net, the amendment would never pass, so they compromised with the moderates and restricted it to race. And in 1870 the Fifteenth Amendment was rat-ified and became part of the Constitution. African-American males now had at least the legal right to vote.

It was a victory for blacks, but paradoxically it ended up much less of a victory than it seemed. Human beings can maintain their intensity for a cause for only so long, especially when it is somebody else's cause. By 1870 the Civil War had been over for five years. During those five years people both North and South had been beset by a whirl of politi-cal, social, and economic problems that needed to be solved. Southerners still had before them the awesome job of rebuilding their society, and just wanted Northerners to leave them alone. Northerners, in their turn, wanted things to get back to normal. Many of them had suffered the loss of husbands, sons, fathers, uncles; and many of those sons and husbands who had survived the war were missing arms and legs. Businessmen in particular wanted things settled so they could do business with Southerners as they had in the past. Indeed, with so much of the South in ruins, there were great opportunities for investment there. How much longer must everybody go on wrangling over Reconstruction and the rights of blacks?

With the Fifteenth Amendment many Northerners breathed a sigh of relief. African-Americans now had the vote; they were strong in many Southern states, the majority in three of them; now, it was thought, they could protect themselves. And so, very quickly, the steam began to go out of the fight for black rights. People in the South realized that Congress and the North in general were growing less interested in protecting the freedmen. Southerners therefore started carrying the battle to the Supreme Court. Through the 1870s and beyond there followed a stream of cases brought by both black and white Southern-ers, asking the Supreme Court to interpret the new laws and constitutional amendments now on the books. What did these laws mean? How should they be applied?

Many of these cases came down to a single question: What powers belonged to the states and what to the Federal government? The question of "states' rights" has dogged the United States from its beginnings and continues to be raised even today. When the thirteen rebellious colonies declared their independence from England in 1776, they took *all* powers that any government might have. But historians debate whether the new states took on the powers individually or as a group in the Continental Congress. But under the Articles of Confederation and then under the new Constitution, which went into effect in 1789, some of the powers of the states were officially and legally transferred to the national govern-ment. (Readers interested in more detail on this important development will find a discussion of it in the volumes in this series called *Creating the*

Constitution and *Building a New Nation*.) Ever since, the question has been whether the Constitution gives the Federal government only a few specific powers, like the right to operate a postal system, raise an army, and make treaties with foreign powers; or does the Constitution by implication give the Federal government broader, indeed sweeping, powers? Generally speaking, the Supreme Court has ruled that the Constitution, by implication, gives the Federal government considerably more power than is actually spelled out. But there have always remained doubts, gray

An unusual view of the State House in Philadelphia, better known as Independence Hall, where the U.S. Constitution was written in 1787. Right from the beginning, one of the biggest arguments at the Constitutional Convention was how much power should be given to the national government, and how much kept by the states. Historians agree that ultimate power was granted to the national government, but there have always been "States' Righters" who insist that the states ought to have the final say.

areas, and fuzzy points. (The Supreme Court dealt with this question in *McCulloch v. Maryland,* which is discussed in the volume, *The Jeffersonian Republicans*, in this series.)

The batch of cases flowing into the Supreme Court during Reconstruction was aimed at these disputed points. The first question asked, just what rights did the Fourteenth Amendment protect? Second, remember that the main thrust of the amendments and Reconstruction acts passed by Congress was to force the Southern states to uphold civil rights for African-Americans. And to enforce the amendments, Congress passed laws to protect people from having their rights violated by private citizens. White Southerners now wanted the Supreme Court to rule that such acts went beyond what the amendments allowed the Federal government to do, intruding on state powers. Blacks and their many white supporters, of course, wanted the Court to rule in the opposite way.

Among the most important cases to come before the Supreme Court at this time were the so-called Slaughterhouse cases. In 1869, in order to make sure that the butchering of animals took place under sanitary conditions, the Louisiana legislature passed a law requiring all butchers to use one slaughterhouse in New Orleans for butchering their livestock. They could no longer butcher meat on their own property. The butchers who did not want to pay to use this one slaughterhouse sued. They claimed that the law deprived them of their rights under the Fourteenth Amendment which, among other things, said, "No State shall . . . deprive any person of life, liberty, or property, without due process of law; nor deny to any person within its jurisdiction the equal protection of the laws." The Slaughterhouse suits had nothing to do with black rights. But they tested the meaning of the Fourteenth Amendment, which did have something to do with black rights.

In making its decision, the Supreme Court raised the whole question of state versus Federal power. It said that Americans had two separate kinds of citizenship: state citizenship and United States citizenship.

United States citizenship included only a small number of rights, like the right to travel from state to state, the right to do business across state lines, the right to protection when traveling abroad or on the high seas, and a few others. All other rights were to be defined by the states. According to the Supreme Court, the Fourteenth Amendment did not transfer responsibility to protect these rights of state citizenship to the Federal government. The amendment, thus, required the Federal courts to protect only the rights belonging to people as citizens of the United States. Though the First Amendment forbids Congress from abridging people's freedoms of speech, press, and assembly, states were still free to do so. These rights are necessary for effective political participation. In the Slaughterhouse cases, the Court ruled that citizens would have to rely on state courts to protect these rights. And, of course, state courts were staffed entirely by white men. This Supreme Court interpretation sharply limited the power of the Federal government to protect people's rights under the Fourteenth Amendment. Citizens—black and white— now would not be able to use it to protect many things that concerned them.

Minutes after the Court handed down its ruling in the Slaughterhouse cases, it handed down a decision about the equal rights for another group—women. As soon as the Fourteenth Amendment with its equal protection clause was ratified, women wondered if it would apply to them. The Court dealt with this question in a case brought by a woman named Myra Bradwell who wanted to be licensed as a lawyer in Illinois. According to Bradwell, the Fourteenth Amendment guaranteed "the equal protection of the law" to any person born in the United States. Women, therefore, had as much right to be lawyers as men.

The Supreme Court disagreed. One of the justices said, "The civil law, as well as nature itself, has always recognized a wide difference in the respective spheres and destinies of man and woman. Man is, or should be, woman's protector and defender. The natural and proper

In the minds of many people the issue of freedom for blacks was mixed with the concerns of other groups, like women and the poor. Susan B. Anthony began as a fighter for temperance, to cut down on drinking. She then became strongly concerned for black rights; but by the time of the Fifteenth Amendment she was more concerned with getting the vote for women.

timidity and delicacy which belongs to the female sex evidently unfits it for many of the occupations of civil life."

This idea may strike us as strange today, but in 1873 it was widely accepted, not only by men but probably the majority of women as well. The decision showed that the Supreme Court would define the rights protected by the Fourteenth Amendment narrowly, leaving the states free to pass almost any laws they wanted. Like the Slaughterhouse cases, the Bradwell case had nothing to do with former slaves, but it had the effect of further limiting the Fourteenth Amendment.

These Supreme Court decisions encouraged whites to believe that they could treat blacks pretty much as they wanted to. African-Americans in the South soon found it difficult to buy first-class tickets on railroad trains and stagecoaches. They were routinely denied the vote through one device or another. One such device was the "grandfather clause," which allowed the right to vote to anyone whose grandfather had voted: The grandfathers of most blacks had been slaves and had not voted. Another device was the poll tax, which had to be paid before you could vote: Many blacks were too poor to pay the poll taxes. (Some Northern states had poll taxes, too, so the effect was to deprive poor people of the vote regardless of their skin color.) Some localities had literacy tests for voters; blacks would be given some complicated material to read, like a legal document, whereas whites were given a newspaper story. If these devices failed, blacks could be intimidated—told they would be beaten if they attempted to vote.

Southern governments passed laws separating the two races, which had the effect of pushing African-Americans into a secondary position. Here a black man on a train is being told to move to a car reserved for blacks. The Civil Rights Act was supposed to prevent this kind of segregation.

Similarly, the schooling of black children was sharply curtailed. Before the Civil War there had been almost no public schools in the South. The Freedmen's Bureau set up schools in many Southern states, and the Republican Reconstruction governments established public school systems. However, as the Southern whites regained control of their states, they weakened their support of public education, especially for black children. In part this was because schools are expensive to run, and Southerners simply did not want to tax themselves to pay for black schools. But part of the idea was to pre-

This cartoon pokes fun at a badly educated Southern white insisting that blacks ought to be literate before they could vote. Southern refusal to spend the necessary money for public schools was partly responsible for keeping this section of the country less prosperous than the rest of the nation.

vent African-Americans from getting educated. All Southern children—especially poor ones—suffered from the curtailing of the school system. But black children suffered worse, for their schools were given much less money than white schools. They were housed in rickety buildings, and had to make do with worn-out textbooks cast off by white schools.

Despite Supreme Court rulings, despite growing Northern indifference to African-Americans' plight, despite the poll taxes and intimidation, the Republican plan for Reconstruction might have held the line on black rights. During this period of the 1870s and the 1880s, there was a surprising amount of racial mixing in the South. Many whites were willing to accept a certain measure of equality for blacks. There were blacks in government, blacks who owned their own farms, blacks doing business with whites in the normal way. If the North had kept the pressure on, it is just possible that blacks would have edged their way step-by-step into the mainstream of Southern society. But there were political movements in the North, too, that would have a major effect in the South.

CHAPTER V

The South Strikes Back

Histry is not made just by great men—kings, presidents, and generals. It is also made by the decisions of millions of ordinary people acting on their own feelings about what they need and want in their lives and the direction they believe their country ought to go in. We cannot really understand what happened in the South after the Civil War until we feel what white Southerners felt. They had been badly defeated in the war, many of their cities in ruins, their homes burned, and their young men dead or crippled. Not only had their lives been ripped apart, but Northern victors were trying to reshape their whole society. They were bitter and resentful. They hated the Northerners who were trying to impose radical ideas on them. And they hated most of all the idea that blacks, whom they had seen for centuries as their inferiors, were to be raised up to equality with them. Indeed, black equality seemed to many white Southerners the very symbol of their defeat. And so the weight of their bitterness and resentment fell heavily on African-Americans.

By the 1870s many Southerners had come to believe that they had a

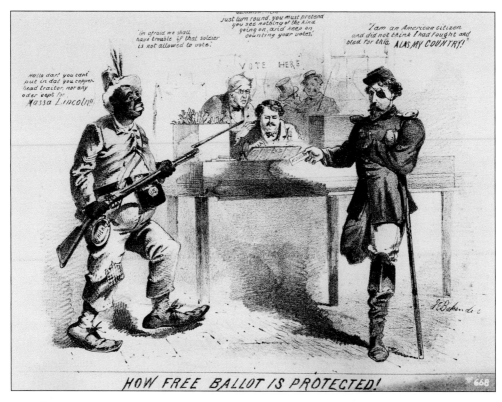

Southern bitterness against the Northern victors was increased by the Federal government's attempts to raise blacks to something like equality with whites. That bitterness is shown in this political cartoon of a satirical black man forcing a Union soldier to vote for Lincoln at gunpoint.

patriotic duty to "redeem" the South—that is, to overturn the Northern victory if they could. That meant putting things back where they had been before the war. Especially it meant putting the bottom rail back on the bottom. And this included the economic side of things, too. Plantation owners, reeling from wartime destruction, needed a cheap labor supply. Keeping control over the freedpeople could serve that purpose. We must understand that, far from feeling guilty about mistreating blacks, the majority of white Southerners, although certainly not all, felt that they were doing the right thing. Was it not a person's duty to redeem himself and his country? Today we find it difficult to accept the attack, of Southern whites of that time on blacks. But we must remember that, had we been in their shoes, we might not have done any better than they.

Southerners found tricks to keep blacks from voting, but the main work of keeping blacks down was done through violence, ranging from threats to outright murder. The most famous instrument of violence, and certainly the most vicious, was an organization known as the Ku Klux Klan. Founded in 1866 as a secret organization, it had passwords, secret codes, costumes, and rituals with mystic significance. The basic goal of the members was to redeem the honor of the South, through violence if necessary. The Klansmen were convinced that they were knights in shining armor fighting a holy war for their country. Very quickly they began to attack blacks, Northern carpetbaggers, and scalawags.

A drawing of Ku Klux Klansmen in their usual costumes. The Klan was eventually broken by Federal judges, but continued to resurface well into the twentieth century.

The Ku Klux Klan was not a well-organized group with orders coming down from an office at the top. It was instead made up of local groups, loosely tied together, following more or less the same ideas and methods. Very quickly the Klan became a powerful force in destroying the effectiveness of the Federal civil rights laws. Klansmen, wearing white-hooded robes to conceal their faces, and carrying guns, came out at night to drag people from their homes to beat them, lash them, shoot them, lynch them from trees, even burn them alive. Most of their victims were black, but they also attacked whites who were trying to help blacks.

John W. Stephens, a white North Carolina politician who had always

This picture shows an incident that took place in 1885 in Northumberland County, Pennsylvania, indicating that the Klan operated in the North as well as the South. The victim is being dragged up and down in an ice-cold stream.

hated the Southern aristocracy, became a Republican leader after the war. He was told again and again that he was risking his life. He replied that three thousand black voters had stood by him, and he had "no idea of abandoning them to the Ku Klux Klan." In 1870 he was murdered.

But it was mostly blacks who bore the brunt of Klan terrorism. Abram Colby, a black leader in Greene County, Georgia, was dragged out of his house while his little daughter begged the Klansmen not to take him away. They took Colby into the woods, stripped him and beat him for three hours—he was lucky to have survived, but his little daughter never got over the shock and died soon after. Andrew Flowers, a black who defeated a white in a Chattanooga election for justice of the peace was whipped in 1870. He said later, "They said they had nothing particular against me, that they didn't dispute I was a very good fellow . . . but they did not intend any nigger to hold office in the United States."

In 1870 a gang of whites broke up a Republican Party rally in Greene County, Alabama, killing four blacks and wounding others. In 1871 in Meridian, Mississippi, Klansmen arrested three African-American leaders for making "incendiary" speeches. During the court hearing there was a shooting. A riot started and about thirty blacks were killed. In Georgia, Washington Eager was murdered because he could read and write, which many of the poorer Southern whites could not. In 1871, in what one historian has called "the most massive Klan action anywhere in the South," five hundred men in hoods broke into a county jail and lynched eight black prisoners. At times the struggle turned into outright warfare.

The members of the Ku Klux Klan were only a minority of Southerners, probably a very small minority. Conversely, not all violence was fomented by the Klansmen. A lot of it was sporadic and unplanned, breaking out when an African-American was elected to some local office or started to become prosperous, and then subsiding when the particular incident was over. Violence against blacks and their white allies tended to be much worse in areas where blacks were a majority or a large minori-

But the bulk of the violence occurred in the South. Here, Klansmen assassinate one of their enemies in Columbus, Georgia.

ty, and thus a greater threat to white control. In some areas, especially in more Northern border states, where blacks were a small percentage of the population, there was relatively little violence, and lynching was a rare occurrence.

Indeed, many Southerners were appalled by the vicious attacks on blacks. But the record shows that all types of people were involved. Abram Colby said that his assailants included men "not worth the bread they eat," but also some of the "first-class men in our town." Another observer said, "The most respectable citizens are engaged in it." It came down to an old truth: While a great many people deplored the violence of the Klan and other groups, they also felt in their hearts that the South had been done an injustice, and that the end justified the means—violence was wrong, but the redemption of the South excused it. A count was not kept until 1882, but from that date to 1916 over three thousand African-American men and women were lynched in the South.

The viciousness of the Klan was too bloody and too obvious to be ignored. Congress passed various acts aimed at the violence, and Federal marshals and district attorneys, backed by Federal power, began to prosecute Klan leaders and others guilty of violence. In some cases, before the troops were withdrawn in 1877, soldiers were used to make arrests, and many of the Klan leaders were jailed. A lot of Klansmen fled their areas and by 1872, says one historian, "the Federal government's evident willingness to bring its legal and coercive authority to bear had broken the Klan's back and produced a dramatic decline in violence throughout the South."

But the lesson had been learned. It was now clear to whites that they could gain control over blacks through violence; and it was clear to blacks that whites would use violence if necessary to keep them down.

By 1875 it had become abundantly clear to the Republicans in Congress that Southerners were managing by trickery and violence to take back from blacks the various civil rights they were supposed to have been guaranteed under the new laws and constitutional amendments. Many Northerners had lost interest in the whole problem, and in March 1875 the dwindling Republican forces pushed through Congress a Civil Rights Act. This basically said that blacks were "entitled to the full and equal enjoyment" of inns, public transportation systems, theaters, and such. It also provided for heavy fines for people who tried to deny blacks these rights.

The Civil Rights Act of 1875 thus was aimed not at Southern *gov-*

ernments but at private individuals—owners of theaters, restaurants, and other facilities. It was based on the Thirteenth Amendment, which had outlawed slavery. The theory behind it was that barring blacks from coaches, theaters, and inns was a "badge of slavery." That is, if you prevented a black person from buying a ticket to a theater, you were treating him like a slave, and slavery was illegal under the Thirteenth Amendment.

Thus matters stood as the presidential election of 1876 rolled around. Andrew Johnson had been president from 1865, when Lincoln was assassinated, until 1868. Johnson, a Tennessee Democrat put on the ticket with Lincoln to draw votes from the border states and Northern Democrats, was by 1868 a man without a party and with very little support among leading politicians and the public generally. In 1868 the Republicans nominated a great war hero, Ulysses S. Grant. Grant, however brilliant a general, proved to be an ineffective president. Among other things, a lot of his officials were corrupt, taking bribes and making deals with businessmen to line their own pockets. Furthermore, although he wanted to see the South reconstructed to a degree, he was only lukewarm about black civil rights. Nonetheless, he had been a hero, and was reelected in 1872.

With the end of Grant's second term in 1876 the Republicans nominated Rutherford B. Hayes. A moderate Republican untouched by the corruption of some of Grant's subordinates, Hayes was wounded in the Civil War, where he had risen to the rank of general. In 1876 he was governor of Ohio. The Democrats nominated Samuel Tilden, governor of New York with a reputation for digging out corruption. Tilden had become rich as a railroad corporation lawyer and was backed by other wealthy businessmen. The Republicans remained strong in the North, and had a good deal of strength in the South, for many blacks were still able to vote and would vote Republican. This was especially true in South Carolina, Florida, and Louisiana, where there were large black populations. The election was close and in the end swung on three states—those same three Southern states. If they all went for Hayes, he would win by one electoral vote. Otherwise Tilden would become president.

The vote in the swing states was in dispute. Both sides had used dirty tactics in the election, and both sides claimed victory in all three states. Congress set up a commission to settle the disputes: seven Republicans, seven Democrats, and a friend of Lincoln's, Supreme Court Justice David Davis, who appeared to be beholden to neither party. In the end Davis was unable to serve. His place was taken by a Republican. The Republicans now had an eight-to-seven majority and, as one might expect, gave all three disputed states to their candidate, Rutherford B. Hayes.

Democrats were incensed, and cried foul. They threatened to prevent the votes from being counted. Looking for a solution, some Republican leaders met with Democratic leaders and made a deal. If the Democrats would let the election of Hayes go through quietly, Hayes would not use the few remaining Federal troops to protect Republicans who claimed to have won state and local offices, or to protect voters in future elections. In their turn, the Southerners pledged to treat African-Americans fairly and respect their rights. The Republicans must have known that the Democratic pledge was meaningless, but they also knew that interest in black civil rights was dwindling, if not already dead, in the North. So the deal was made. Hayes became president.

By now, step-by-step through the South, the radical Reconstruction governments had been replaced by what were called "Redeemer" governments, run by white Democrats determined to return Southern society to what it had been before the war. A few states, like Tennessee and Virginia, had never really been taken over by the radicals. By the time of the Hayes victory, only South Carolina, Florida, and Louisiana still had Republican governments and were, in the eyes of Southerners, unre-

Rutherford B. Hayes became president in a disputed election, when Democrats and Republicans made a deal that would give the South a free hand in dealing with the freedmen and other matters. Effectively, his election ended Reconstruction.

deemed. And in 1877, when President Hayes promised to stop using the small number of Federal troops remaining in the South, Reconstruction was effectively over.

Nonetheless, the laws of the United States said that blacks were to be treated as equal citizens. As Redeemer governments began to take hold in more and more states of the old Confederacy, white Southern politicians were emboldened to challenge the laws Congress had passed to protect civil and political rights.

When African-Americans tried to exercise their rights under the Civil Rights Act of 1875, the Supreme Court ruled the act unconstitutional. Refusing to sell a theater ticket to an African-American had "nothing to do with slavery," the Supreme Court said. "It would be running the slavery argument into the ground to make it apply to every act of discrimination which a person may see fit to make as to the guests he will entertain or as to the people he will take into his coach or cab or car, or admit to his concert or theater or deal with in other matters of intercourse or business . . . ." In other words, according to the Supreme Court, state governments might not be permitted to discriminate against blacks, but private citizens, like owners of inns, taverns, or theaters could.

Other Court decisions had the effect of leaving the regulation of almost all activity in the hands of the by now once again thoroughly white state governments. Thus, if African-Americans were discriminated against by white legislators, their only recourse was to the state courts staffed by white judges. Many of these men were former slave owners: None of them saw black Americans as equal in any way to white Americans.

CHAPTER VI

The South "Redeemed"

Despite everything, blacks had made some gains during the Reconstruction era. Schools were segregated, but most other areas of Southern life were not—at least, not by law. Generally speaking, blacks and whites lived together in the same neighborhoods. They mingled in some theaters and restaurants, and in many places blacks had the vote. This mixing of whites and blacks was more common in the older southeastern states, but it existed to a degree everywhere in the South. But by local custom blacks and whites were kept separate in most facilities.

However, by 1877 Redeemer governments had taken over in all the Southern states and the Northern troops were mostly gone. Over the years through to the end of the century, by various means, whites pushed blacks step-by-step further back into serfdom.

There was more to the story than that, however, for not only were blacks driven into a grinding poverty, but so were a great many whites. The net result was that while the rest of the United States was expanding westward, and growing rich from the rapidly developing industrial system, the South remained the poorest section of the nation, a place with high rates of illiteracy, relatively little manufacturing, a lot of disease, and malnutrition. (For an account of post–Civil War industry see the volume in this series called *The Rise of Industrial America*.)

Two trends in the years after the Civil War were mainly responsible for keeping much of the South in poverty. The first was the return to power of the Southern conservatives—the big plantation owners who had controlled the South politically and economically before the war—and their new allies among businessmen and lawyers. As we have seen, these big planters had been heartily disliked by many of the small farmers who made up so much of the population of the South. Some of these small farmers, working in alliance with black voters, had helped Republicans to curb the aristocrats in some states. But after 1877 the old traditional leaders were again in power in most states. Once they had rendered the Republican Party powerless in their states, they managed to get and keep political office by gaining the votes of freedmen—in some cases their former slaves. They did this by putting African-Americans on the ballot for low-level offices and appointing them to many government jobs. Because of their larger numbers of black residents, areas where the plantation aristocrats dominated sent more representatives to the state legislatures than other regions. Thus the old planter aristocracy was able to reassert its authority over the poor whites as well as blacks by getting the black vote.

At first some poor whites thought they could combine with poor blacks to defeat the old aristocracy. But the planters were in office and could give jobs to black leaders and hold the votes of African-Americans. At the same time, they divided poor whites by appealing to racism. Finally, many poor whites concluded that they could only defeat the aristocracy by depriving them of the black vote. They began a campaign to disfranchise African-Americans, that is, take the vote away from them. The men already in power then joined the antiblack political movement

Main Street of a small Southern town after the Civil War: the street is dirt, the buildings ramshackle and long-unpainted. Sharecropping and the dominance of a small minority of wealthy planters, who wanted to keep things unchanged, mired the South in poverty while the North grew prosperous on industry.

rather than appear to favor black rights. Each group tried to see who could be more antiblack in order to get white votes. At the same time, Southern state legislatures began their efforts to legally disfranchise the African-Americans.

The by now nearly all-white legislatures pushed for laws limiting the vote to people who paid a special tax on each adult, called a poll tax; and they required potential voters to demonstrate the ability to read. Such laws kept out of the polling almost all African-Americans, as well as a lot of poor white men who were illiterate. Poor white farmers, then, could no more get themselves elected to office, in order to protect their rights, any more than blacks could. Thus, through a whole variety of political devices, by the 1880s the aristocrats were coming back into power.

A second tendency helping to keep the South in poverty was the rise of the sharecropping system. Even before the end of the Civil War there was much talk of breaking up the large plantations in order to give freedmen the "forty acres and a mule" they thought they had been promised. Many radical Republicans wanted to do this; and by the end of the war blacks generally believed it would happen. It did begin to happen, in a few places during the war.

But there was a great deal of feeling, in the North as well as the South, against taking people's property away. Didn't the Constitution say that Congress could not take anyone's property without "due process of law"? So the plan was never really tried, and the lands were taken away from the freedmen and given back to their former owners.

With the end of the war, blacks were no longer slaves, but were free to take jobs where they wanted. The Black Codes, however, put sharp limits on that freedom, requiring blacks to sign contracts to go to work for plantation owners, often on the very farms where they had labored as slaves.

Blacks balked at this. They wanted their own cabins where they could live with their families, they wanted to farm their land for themselves. In the early days of Reconstruction, when Republican governments were forming, and the Freedmen's Bureau had much power in the South, a new system of labor for Southern plantations was worked out—sharecropping. In this system each black family was allotted a certain piece of land on which to grow a crop, usually cotton. Here the family could construct its own cabin and live apart from other families. The white owner usually provided seeds, fertilizer, a mule, and tools, although in some instances the black sharecropper got these things for himself. At harvest time the crop would be divided, often into thirds: one-third to the sharecropper,

This picture of a sharecropper's cabin was taken in about 1900, and shows a dwelling that was probably better than earlier sharecropper cabins had been. Sharecroppers — black and white — typically went barefoot and dressed in ragged clothes, as this picture shows.

one-third to the landowner, and one-third to whoever provided seeds, fertilizer, and the mule.

In the sharecropping system blacks got some advantage from their labor: If they worked harder they would grow a larger crop and come out at the end of the year with more money. Even more important, they could develop family lives for themselves away from the gaze of the whites.

White landowners, too, favored the sharecropping system, for it meant that when prices went down and cash was short, they did not have to pay out wages for their black workers. The system also encouraged blacks to work harder than they might have just for wages. Sharecropping very rapidly became the basic farm labor system in the South. In time many poor white farmers became sharecroppers, too.

But in the long run the sharecropping system proved to be disastrous for the South as a whole. As it worked out, the people who benefited from it most were the merchants in local communities who sold the planters the seed, fertilizer, and tools they needed to run their farms. In the spring the landowner would buy his supplies from the merchant on credit, usually at very high rates of interest. In the fall, if all went well, he would pay off the debt, and have a little profit left over. But sometimes all did not go well. The crop might not flourish due to bad weather. Prices might fall, as they did when the war ended and wartime demand for cotton stopped. In such cases the landowner might not have enough money from the sale of his cotton to pay his debt. Debts could, and did, pile up year after year, until the landowner might be forced to sell his farm and become a sharecropper himself. This happened thousands of times under sharecropping. Frequently the merchants ended up owning much of the land in their communities.

For black farmers, the system was even worse than it was for the small landowner. They often had to buy the very food they ate on credit from the local merchant while the unedible cash crop—usually cotton or tobacco—grew. If the crop was good and the price was high, they might end the year a little ahead. But too often things did not go well, and sharecroppers were forced to go on borrowing. They became trapped in a cycle of debt year after year, from which they could escape only by fleeing in the night—and starting the cycle all over again someplace else.

Quite early, many thoughtful Southerners saw the problems in the sharecropping system. They believed that Southern farmers ought first to

*Another picture from around 1900 shows the extent of Southern poverty;
This couple does not even own a mule, much less a tractor, to pull the primi-
tive wooden plow, but tugs it through the hard earth by hand.*

make themselves self-sufficient by growing their own food—corn, veg-
etables, hogs, chickens—instead of only cotton. If the farmers could at
least feed themselves and grow a little cotton on the side to bring in some
cash for their taxes and the few things they had to buy, they might escape
from the cycle of debt.

But there was a problem with that. The local Southern merchants needed cash to pay off their own debts, and buy goods for their stores, for many of them were, in turn, in debt to Northern merchants and bankers. Cotton could be sold quickly for cash, whereas there was nothing for the merchant to sell if the farmers were eating their crops. Merchants therefore told landowners and sharecroppers that they would only sell them goods on credit if they planted cotton.

Some landowners came to realize that they could escape from the debt cycle if they became merchants themselves, buying seed, corn, pork, and tools directly from big suppliers. Sharecroppers then were forced to buy their food from the landowners. They would end up being permanently in debt to the landowners. In these situations the sharecroppers were effectively back in slavery, with this one difference: Their families could not be broken up and sold away.

In the end, the system worked to keep not just blacks but the entire South from developing. Blacks in particular, but poor whites, too, went uneducated, and could not find ways to advance themselves. The whole economy was trapped in a cycle of poverty by debt and ignorance. One expert has said, "The rural South of 1900 was stagnant. Crop outputs, yields per acre, and agricultural technology remained virtually the same year after year. Progress was nowhere in evidence."

However bad things were for poor whites, they were always worse for blacks. Throughout the 1880s and 1890s the whites step-by-step forced blacks back into a peonage that was far short of the equal freedom that so much blood had been spilled to secure. At the same time white Southerners established the policy known as "Jim Crow," a derisive term taken from the stage name of a white entertainer who did a comic imitation of a dance he had seen done by a crippled old black man.

The object of the Jim Crow laws was to separate the races—to segregate blacks into their own sections of railroad and trolley cars, their own theaters and restaurants. The Southern schools, such as they were, had been segregated from their start at the end of the war. The real idea was

Violence against blacks in the South, and to a lesser extent in the North, continued through the nineteenth century and into the twentieth century. Here, during the so-called Patenburg massacre of 1872, white men attack a black man with stones and clubs.

to achieve "white supremacy." The bottom rail was to be kept on the bottom, after all. Private institutions and businesses were theoretically free to do as they wished, but state legislatures passed laws requiring them to serve either whites or blacks, but not the two together. Thus while in theory black schools, theaters, and restaurants were "separate but equal," in fact they were always separate, but rarely equal.

Segregation was not just a system of separation; it was a system of domination.

Most particularly, blacks were not allowed to vote. Theoretically, they could: The Fifteenth Amendment said so. But with Mississippi taking the lead, state after state adopted devices to screen out blacks at the voting place, through literacy tests, the poll tax, grandfather clauses, or outright intimidation. Blacks were soon disfranchised. For example, in Louisiana in 1896 there were 130,340 registered black voters; in 1904 there were 1,342.

The final straw came in 1896 with the famous case of *Plessy v. Ferguson*. Homer A. Plessy got on a railroad train and sat in the white area to test the Louisiana Jim Crow laws. He was arrested, and took the case to the Supreme Court under the Fourteenth Amendment, which guaranteed all citizens equal protection of the law. In its decision the court said that the intention of the Fourteenth Amendment "was undoubtedly to enforce the absolute equality of the two races before the law." Then it went on to say, "but in the nature of things it could not have been intended to abolish distinctions based on color." It added, segregation did not "necessarily imply the inferiority of either race to the other." Only one of the nine justices disagreed with this opinion. Justice John Marshall Harlan in his dissent said, "Our Constitution is color-blind, and neither knows nor tolerates classes among citizens." But Harlan's was a lonely voice; the majority believed otherwise, and pronounced it legal for states to separate the races in all sorts of ways.

Ironically, not all Southerners were pleased, for segregation was costly. It meant that small towns had to build two jails instead of one, railroad and trolley companies had to have extra cars for blacks. In Kentucky, for instance, a small integrated college founded just before the war was forced to choose to serve either white or black students; it chose to stay open for whites only. Such acts became common all across the South. Segregation now had the support of the U.S. Constitution.

Justice John Marshall Harlan was the only member of the Supreme Court in the famous Plessy *case to insist that segregation implied inequality.*

Historians today agree that the Supreme Court decision in *Plessy v. Ferguson* was simply wrong: Segregation did imply inferiority. In 1954, in another famous case, *Brown v. Board of Education*, the Supreme Court said just that, and reversed *Plessy*, opening the door for vast change in the status of African-Americans. But in 1896 the men on the Supreme Court, along with the majority of Americans, refused to believe that enforced segregation was in its very nature unequal. And with *Plessy*, black hope for equality was finished for half a century.

Reconstruction and its aftermath is one of the saddest eras in American history. It is true that during the first years of Reconstruction a lot of good-hearted white Americans tried very hard to help bring African-Americans into real citizenship. And despite the considerable violence used against blacks, many Southerners, however reluctantly, saw that times had changed and were willing to tolerate a measure of equality for blacks. Had Northern whites continued to press hard for black equality, undoubtedly blacks would have gained a lot of their civil rights—although perhaps not full equality, for there was too much resistance in the South for that.

But Northern whites got tired of the struggle, which after all did not affect them personally. Southern whites believed that it *did* affect them personally and went on fighting until they had won.

Or so it seemed. But in fact, Jim Crow hurt all of America. By keeping much of the Southern population—white and black—in poverty and ignorance, it prevented the South from developing both economically and socially. And in holding back a great section of the nation, it held back the nation as a whole.

Justice Harlan's viewpoint eventually prevailed, when in 1954, the Supreme Court under Chief Justice Earl Warren (seated, center) ruled that separation did in fact imply inequality.

BIBLIOGRAPHY

*Many of the books that are no longer in print may still be found
in School or Public Libraries.*

For Students:

Mettger, Zak. *Reconstruction: America After the Civil War.* New York:
Lodestar Books, 1994.

Smith, C. Carter, ed. *One Nation Again: A Sourcebook on the Civil War.*
Brookfield, CT: Millbrook Press, 1993.

Stalcup, Brenda, ed. *Reconstruction: Opposing Viewpoints.* San Diego:
Greenhaven Press, 1995.

For Teachers:

Douglass, Frederick. *Narrative of the Life of Frederick Douglass, an American
Slave, Written by Himself.* Edited by David W. Blight. Boston: Bedford
Books, 1993.

Foner, Eric. *Reconstruction: America's Unfinished Revolution, 1863–1877.*
New York: Harper and Row, 1989.

Franklin, John Hope. *Reconstruction After the Civil War.* 2d ed. Chicago: University of Chicago Press, 1995.

Ransom, Roger L., and Richard Sutch. *One Kind of Freedom: The Economic Consequence of Emancipation.* Cambridge: Cambridge University Press, 1977.

Rose, Willie Lee. *Rehearsal for Reconstruction: The Port Royal Experiment.* Indianapolis: Bobbs-Merrill, 1967.

Woodward, C. Vann. *The Strange Career of Jim Crow.* 3d rev. ed. New York: Oxford University Press, 1974.

INDEX

JAMES LINCOLN COLLIER is the author of a number of books both for adults and for young people, including the social history *The Rise of Selfishness in America*. He is also noted for his biographies and historical studies in the field of jazz. Together with his brother, Christopher Collier, he has written a series of award-winning historical novels for children widely used in schools, including the Newbery Honor classic, *My Brother Sam Is Dead*. A graduate of Hamilton College, he lives with his wife in New York City.

CHRISTOPHER COLLIER grew up in Fairfield County, Connecticut and attended public schools there. He graduated from Clark University in Worcester, Massachusetts and earned M.A. and Ph.D. degrees at Columbia University in New York City. After service in the Army and teaching in secondary schools for several years, Mr. Collier began teaching college in 1961. He is now Professor of History at the University of Connecticut and Connecticut State Historian. Mr. Collier has published many scholarly and popular books and articles about Connecticut and American history. With his brother, James, he is the author of nine historical novels for young adults, the best known of which is *My Brother Sam Is Dead*. He lives with his wife Bonnie, a librarian, in Orange, Connecticut.

DATE DUE

NOV 1 5 2001

MAY 1 3 2002

MAR 0 7 2003

ILL # 351058 PPN

MAY 0 5 2005

PRINTED IN U.S.A.

GAYLORD